ENDIKE PRIMARY SCHOOL
ENDIKE LANE
HULL
HU6 7UR
TEL: 01482 616461

Looking *at* Pictures

In the Distance
~ Joy Richardson ~

FRANKLIN WATTS
LONDON • NEW YORK • SYDNEY

© 1997 Franklin Watts

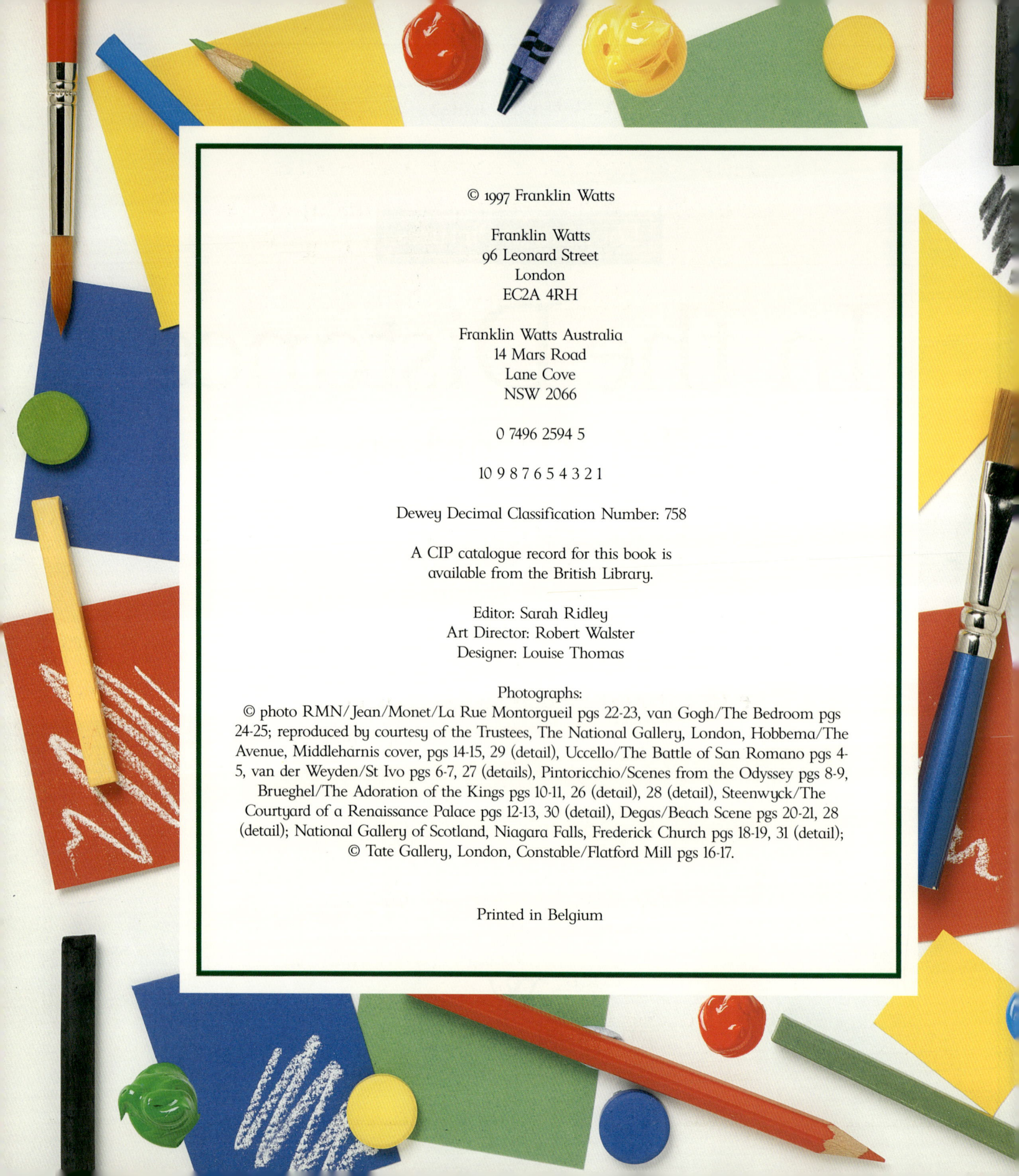

Franklin Watts
96 Leonard Street
London
EC2A 4RH

Franklin Watts Australia
14 Mars Road
Lane Cove
NSW 2066

0 7496 2594 5

10 9 8 7 6 5 4 3 2 1

Dewey Decimal Classification Number: 758

A CIP catalogue record for this book is available from the British Library.

Editor: Sarah Ridley
Art Director: Robert Walster
Designer: Louise Thomas

Photographs:
© photo RMN/Jean/Monet/La Rue Montorgueil pgs 22-23, van Gogh/The Bedroom pgs 24-25; reproduced by courtesy of the Trustees, The National Gallery, London, Hobbema/The Avenue, Middleharnis cover, pgs 14-15, 29 (detail), Uccello/The Battle of San Romano pgs 4-5, van der Weyden/St Ivo pgs 6-7, 27 (details), Pintoricchio/Scenes from the Odyssey pgs 8-9, Brueghel/The Adoration of the Kings pgs 10-11, 26 (detail), 28 (detail), Steenwyck/The Courtyard of a Renaissance Palace pgs 12-13, 30 (detail), Degas/Beach Scene pgs 20-21, 28 (detail); National Gallery of Scotland, Niagara Falls, Frederick Church pgs 18-19, 31 (detail); © Tate Gallery, London, Constable/Flatford Mill pgs 16-17.

Printed in Belgium

Contents

*How do you fill a room with space,
or make a road lead into the distance,
all in a thin layer of paint?*

Explore the pictures in this book
to discover some artists' answers.

 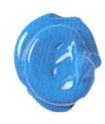  

The Battle of San Romano 4
St. Ivo 6
Scenes from the Odyssey 8
The Adoration of the Kings 10
The Courtyard of a Renaissance Palace 12
The Avenue, Middelharnis 14
Flatford Mill 16
Niagara Falls 18
Beach Scene 20
La Rue Montorgueil 22
The Bedroom 24
Near and Far 26
More about the pictures in this book 30
Index 32

The Battle of San Romano
painted by Uccello

Uccello enjoyed working out how to paint things to look close by or further away.

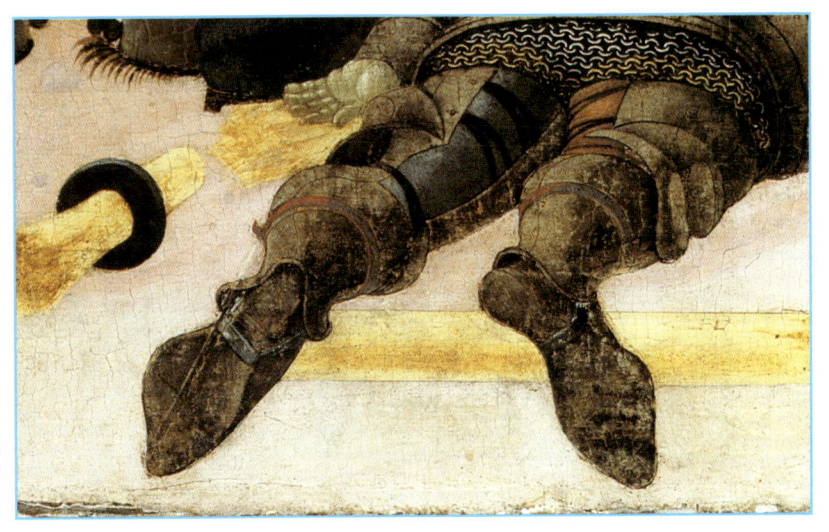

These feet look big sticking out towards you in the foreground.

Look at the size of the horses in front and these galloping away into the distance.

Uccello makes faraway trees look smaller and paler.

St. Ivo
painted by van der Weyden

You can zoom backwards
and forwards in this picture
to focus on the man or the view outside.

The man fills the foreground, reading this writing.

Take a look through the window at life outside.

Follow the horse up the path to the castle.

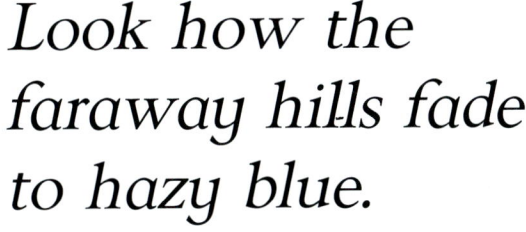

Look how the faraway hills fade to hazy blue.

Scenes from the Odyssey
painted by Pintoricchio

Penelope weaves and waits for Odysseus
to come home from the wars.
Here he is at last.

Look at all the lines
leading towards
the window.

The hero's ship and the distant
sea help to tell
the story.

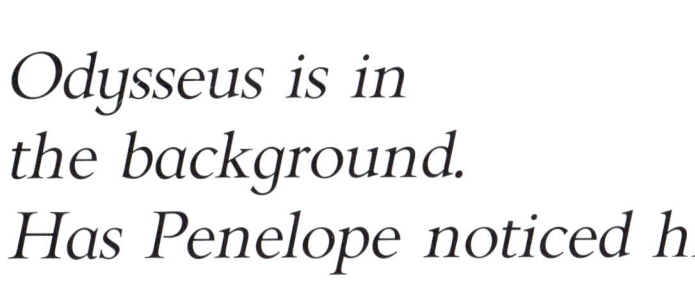

Odysseus is in
the background.
Has Penelope noticed him yet?

The Adoration of the Kings
painted by Brueghel the Elder

People crowd into the picture
as the Kings bring gifts to Jesus.

The rickety stable fills half the picture.

You can see a whole town in the background.

There are people everywhere. How many can you count?

Faces look smaller at the back of the crowd.

People grow fainter in the distance.

The Courtyard of a Renaissance Palace
painted by van Steenwyck

The painter lines everything up
to give you a perfect view
of this imaginary palace.

Follow the straight lines back into the picture. They all lead your eyes to the far archway.

Pillars shrink on the way.

You can see up into this room.

Light and shade shape the steps.

The Avenue, Middelharnis
painted by Hobbema

Hobbema liked the pattern of the trees lining this road into the town.

The road and the trees make triangle shapes pointing into the distance.

How far apart are these people?

Sky meets earth at the low horizon.

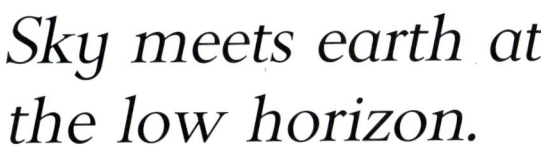

Trees soar high against the sky.

Flatford Mill
painted by Constable

Constable knew every inch
of this river as a child.
His eyes sucked it into his memory.

What is this horse pulling?

Glimpse the river again around the corner.

Walk your eyes along the towpath. Who do you meet?

Look at the clouds stacked above the horizon.

Niagara Falls
painted by Church

Rushing, tumbling, spraying water fills the picture as far as the eye can see.

Look right across to the
far bank of the river.

Watch the water
tumbling over the edge.

People are watching.
Tiny figures show
the size of the
waterfall.

Where does the rainbow start?

Beach Scene
painted by Degas

Degas painted the hair-combing indoors, in his studio, and then filled in a beach background.

Look at the high horizon. How much of the picture is sea and sky?

Hands comb hair carefully in the middle of the picture.

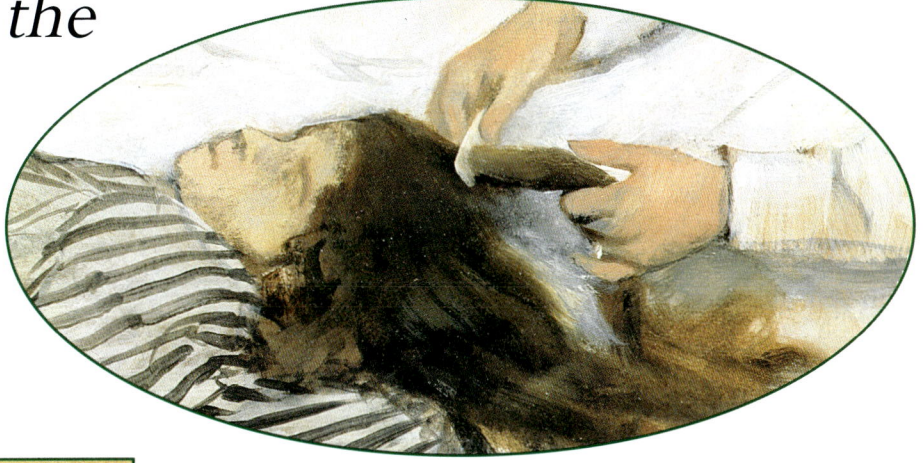

Scattered objects look large in the foreground.

Black blobs make distant bathers.

La Rue Montorgueil
painted by Monet

It is festival day in Paris. Flags deck the buildings. Crowds gather in the street.

You seem to be high up looking down.
How far along the street can you see?

Nearer buildings look taller.

Flags grow smaller
down the street.

Look how the crowds of
people are painted.

The Bedroom
painted by van Gogh

Van Gogh loved this simple room
in a house he had rented.

The closer end of the bed is painted much bigger than the other end.

Which chair leg is nearest?

Light changes the colour where the walls meet.

Look how the table's square corners seem to change shape.

Near and Far

Changing sizes

Things which are near you look big. Faraway things look smaller.

Try drawing a person in the foreground with buildings or trees in the background. Look carefully to make the sizes show how far away things are.

For help, look back at pages 4 and 10.

Through the window

Try making a near and far picture. Paint a wall with a window or an open door and the view you can see through it.

For help, look back at pages 6 and 8.

Faraway colours

Have you noticed how colours often look lighter and hazier a long way away?

Mix colours carefully to paint a picture with water, hills or buildings in the far distance.

For help, look at pages 4, 6 and 10.

On the horizon

The sky seems to come right down to meet the earth at the horizon.

Look out of the window and paint what you can see where the sky meets the earth. You can choose to put the horizon low or high in your picture.

For help, look at pages 14, 16 and 20.

Crowd control

Try painting a picture with lots of people.
Make the people bigger in front and smaller behind.
Distant people need less detail.

For help, look back at pages 10, 20 and 22.

Meeting points

If you look straight ahead along a road or a corridor, the sides seem to lead inwards in the distance.

High lines, like the tops of trees, seem to lead down. Low lines, like the edge of the road, seem to lead up into the distance.

Look straight ahead along a path or down a corridor. Try drawing what you see, showing lines leading into the distance

For help, look at pages 14, 22 and 24.

More about the pictures in this book

■ The Battle of San Romano

Paolo Uccello (1397-1475) lived in Florence. This painting, showing victory in a skirmish against Siena, was made to decorate the palace of the ruling Medici family. Uccello loved working out perspective, as seen in the foreshortened knight, the arrangement of lances on the ground and even the measurements of the big red hat.

■ St. Ivo

Rogier van der Weyden (about 1400-1464) was Flemish and became the official painter to the city of Brussels. Saint Ivo was the patron saint of lawyers, and stood up for the poor. In this painting he is probably reading a legal document, while daily life goes on in the background.

■ Scenes from the Odyssey

Bernardino di Betto Pintoricchio (about 1454-1513) was Italian. He painted this picture on plaster to decorate a wall in the royal palace in Siena. It shows a scene from the story of the *Odyssey*. Odysseus returned from the Trojan Wars after ten years of adventures and killed off the suitors who had been wooing his waiting wife.

■ The Adoration of the Kings

Jan Brueghel the Elder (1568-1625) belonged to a famous family of Flemish painters. His paintings are filled with detail from his own time. This interesting scene shows kings and shepherds, a crowd of on-lookers and a whole Flemish town in the background.

■ The Courtyard of a Renaissance Palace

Hendrick van Steenwyck (about 1580-1649) was Flemish but lived in Frankfurt, London and the Netherlands. He specialised in painting the architecture of buildings. This fantasy picture shows off his mastery of perspective. All the lines along steps, balustrades and floor tiles seem to lead back to the same point in the distance, known as the 'vanishing point'. The people were painted in afterwards by someone else. You can see through the paint in places.

◼ The Avenue, Middelharnis

Meindert Hobbema (1638-1709) lived in Holland. He gave up professional painting when he was thirty to go into the wine business. Twenty years later, on a visit to southern Holland, he saw this avenue of tall bare trees soaring into the sky and thought what a good picture it would make. It became his best known work.

◼ Flatford Mill

John Constable (1776-1837) grew up in Suffolk, England. His father owned the mill at Flatford on the River Stour which appears in this painting. Constable drew inspiration from the familiar scenes of his childhood. He wanted to show nature truthfully in all its simple beauty.

◼ Niagara Falls

Frederick Edwin Church (1826-1900) was an American landscape painter. He liked painting nature in the dramatic, breathtaking forms of waterfalls, rainbows, storms and icebergs. This painting shows the Niagara Falls from the American side with Canada across the river.

◼ Beach Scene

Hilaire-Germaine-Edgar Degas (1834-1917) was one of the group of French painters who became known as impressionists. Unlike some of his friends, he preferred painting indoors. He posed the nursemaid combing the girl's hair in his studio. He painted in the golden beach to make a good background.

◼ La Rue Montorgueil

Claude Monet (1840-1926) was the best known of all the French impressionists for his exploration of the effects of light and colour, as seen in this painting. It captures the joyfulness of a holiday celebrating the Universal Exhibition in Paris in 1878.

◼ The Bedroom

Vincent van Gogh (1853-90) rented the 'Yellow House' at Arles in the south of France in 1888. He painted this room to celebrate his new, settled life. He thought it was one of his best pictures, strong and simple, and later painted two more copies of it.

Index

battle 4-5
beach 20-1
Brueghel the Elder 10, 30
buildings 10, 11, 12-13, 23, 26

Church 18, 31
colours 5, 7, 25, 27
Constable 16, 31

Degas 20, 31

foreground 5, 7, 21, 26
furniture 25

Hobbema 14, 31
horizon 15, 17, 21, 28
horses 5, 7, 17

light 13, 25
lines and meeting points 13, 15, 29

Monet 22, 31

people and crowds 5, 6, 7, 9, 10, 11, 15, 17, 19, 20, 21, 22, 23, 26, 28

Pintoricchio 8, 30

rainbow 19
rivers 16, 17, 19
roads and streets 14, 15, 22-3, 29
rooms 8-9, 13, 24-5

sea 9, 21
sizes, changing 26
sky and clouds 15, 17, 21, 28

trees 5, 14, 15, 26, 29

Uccello 4, 5, 30

van der Weyden 6, 30
van Gogh 24, 31
van Steenwyck 12, 30
views 6, 7, 27

water 16, 17, 18-19
windows 7, 9, 27